Blockchain Security Analysis

A POMDP-Based Approach for Analyzing Blockchain System Security Against the Long Delay Attack

Yuan Liu
Shuangfeng Zhang
Xingren Chen
Xin Zhou
Xin Zheng

ELIVA PRESS

ELIVA PRESS

Yuan Liu
Shuangfeng Zhang
Xingren Chen
Xin Zhou
Xin Zheng

Blockchain is a distributed ledger, offering an innovative approach to establishing trust in a public and open environment. However, it bears many security attacks in sustaining data/status consistency in the process of data storing and exchanging, and the long-delay attack is one of the most challenging ones. Many researchers have adopted various methods in analyzing the blockchain system security by considering a upper-bounded and static network latency. In a realistic scenario, the network latency is always changing dynamically, resulting in the unreliability and inaccuracy of the existing analysis approaches. In this book, we propose a blockchain security analysis model based on partially observable Markov decision process (POMDP) against the long delay attack by capturing the dynamic network delay. In our model, an observation function about the network delay is learned and updated based on a clustering algorithm according to the real-time network status. With the support of the observation function, a POMDP model is constructed for attackers to maximize their expected rewards. To analyze the security of a blockchain system against the long delay attack, the utility of the attackers and normal miners with the same mining power is calculated and compared. The system is safe as the utility of the normal miners is no less than that of the attackers. Extensive experiments are conducted to show the effectiveness of the proposed analysis model, where Bitcoin system is evaluated and the safe ranges of the system network parameters are analyzed.

Published: Eliva Press SRL
Address: MD-2060, bd.Cuza-Voda, 1/4, of. 21 Chişinău, Republica Moldova
Email: info@elivapress.com
Website: www.elivapress.com

ISBN: 978-1-952751-33-2

ABSTRACT

Blockchain is a distributed ledger, offering an innovative approach to establishing trust in a public and open environment, which has been regarded as the supporting technical architecture to the future distributed applications (DApps). However, it bears many security attacks in sustaining data/status consistency in the process of data storing and exchanging, and the long-delay attack is one of the most challenging ones. Many researchers have adopted various methods in analyzing the blockchain system security by considering a upper-bounded and static network latency. In a realistic scenario, the network latency is always changing dynamically, resulting in the unreliability and inaccuracy of the existing analysis approaches. In this paper, we propose a blockchain security analysis model based on partially observable Markov decision process (POMDP) against the long delay attack by capturing the dynamic network delay. In our model, an observation function about the network delay is learned and updated based on a clustering algorithm according to the real-time network status. With the support of the observation function, a POMDP model is constructed for attackers to maximize their expected rewards. To analyze the security of a blockchain system against the long delay attack, the utility of the attackers and normal miners with the same mining power is calculated and compared. The system is safe as the utility of the normal miners is no less than that of the attackers. Extensive experiments are conducted to show

1

the effectiveness of the proposed analysis model, where Bitcoin system is evaluated and the safe ranges of the system network parameters are analyzed.

1. INTRODUCTION

A blockchain system is a distributed ledger to record data in an immutable manner [1, 2]. With its distinguishing characteristics, such as decentralization, nonrepudiation, traceability, and transparency [3], the blockchain technology has attracted many attentions in various fields, such as finance [4], healthcare [5], e-governance [6]. A blockchain network achieves the data consistent status through a consensus protocol, such as proof of work (PoW) in BitCoin [1]. The analysis of a consensus protocol against various attacking behaviors has been extensively studied, where the network delay is widely recognized to be a significant parameter [7, 8, 9].

Network delay is an unavoidable phenomena when information is transferred in an asynchronized network[10, 11]. For example, in PoW consensus mechanism of BitCoin, every new block broadcast in the network will cause propagation delay. The propagation delay consists of transmission time[12] and local validation time. Usually, it takes nearly 10 seconds from a single node publishing a block to the whole blockchain system reaching the consensus [13]. Such a long time delay could result in a high risk of forking and cause the wastes of miners' computing resources [15, 14]. Unfortunately, this factor has not been paid sufficient attentions to analyzing blockchain system security before the formalization of the long delay attack [13]. The long delay attack was first formally proposed in a generalized asynchronous environment, where the attackers delay the message transmission between honest miners to earn relatively

3

longer mining time by starting mining the next block in advance. Thus, the attackers can achieve a higher probability in successfully mining the next block [7]. The authors [13] further enriched the delay attack by extending the network delay from a fixed boundary to a flexible settting. However, it is noteworthy that these studies do not consider the impact of the dynamic changes of network latency on the system security analysis. A natural question we are interested in is how to analyze the security of a blockchain system against the long delay attack when the network delay is dynamically changing.

In this study, we aim to provide a POMDP-based security analysis approach for blockchain systems against the long delay attack. In our analysis, the attackers performing the long delay attack are rational and always try their best to maximize their mining rewards. As the network delay is a partially observed system parameter and directly affect the attacking success rate of their attackers, we constructed a POMDP-based model for attackers in making their attacking decisions. The network latency is observed as the time difference between information being transmitted and being received, and a belief function is then built and updated based on a clustering method. With the support of the POMDP model, the attackers are able to adjust their attacking strategy and achieve their maximal expected rewards. By comparing the rewards of the attackers with the honest miners, the security of the blockchain system against the long delay attack is conclusive. Specifically, the system is regarded to be safe against the long delay attack if the attackers' rewards are no more than the honest miners, and vice versa.

4

We make the following contributions in this work:

- A POMDP model is constructed for attackers to optimize their long-delay attacking strategy, where the six main components are specified.

- The network delay is observed and characterized by employing a clustering algorithm so that the dynamic network status is accurately updated with time.

- A security analysis method is proposed to evaluate whether a blockchain system is safe against the long delay attack.

- Through experimental evaluation in BitCoin blockchain systems, we can learn the crucial parameters influencing system security and their safe value domains, which potentially suggest how to improve the design of a blockchain system towards secure and efficient systems.

2. RELATED WORK

2.1. Security of blockchain systems

Since the birth of BitCoin [1] by Nakamoto in 2008, the blockchain technology has been developing rapidly in both academic and industry [3]. Many application platforms and architectures for blockchain have been launched, such as Ethereum1, Hyperledger [16]. A series of research studies analyze the security of blockchain applications in various attacking scenarios. The attacks are explicitly discussed. For example, the double-spending attack means that the attackers use the same currency in two different transactions in the same blockchain system. The selfish mining attack refers to the case where the miners try to selectively withholding their blocks and only publishing them gradually to increase their expected benefits in the process of mining [17]. Both of the two attacks require the adversaries to master a relatively large number of miners or mining power, which makes these attacks bear high cost in reality. Instead of attempting to corrupt a sizable fraction of miners, it would be much easier for the adversary to disrupt communications among miners through performing delays. To differentiate this type of attacks from the former two, it is also regarded as non-power-based attack [18].

Many researchers thus have shifted their attentions from the attacking with massive mining power to disrupting communication between miners. The long delay attack is firstly proposed in [7], where the adversaries try to delay the delivery of messages as much as possible when transferring messages between 80 miners. In this way, the adversaries obtain a relatively longer mining time for himself. The effect of this attack is that it increases the difficulty of other honest miners in mining a new block and reduces the mining difficulty for the adversaries themselves at the same time. The long delay attack is then enriched by Wei et al [13]. After receiving the miner's blocks, an adversary can choose an effective chain he wants to delay with a certain success rate. After a successful delay attack, those delayed chains are marked as *delayed*, while others are marked as *non-delayed*. The purpose of this approach is to alert the adversaries to send messages within the network latency bound. The adversaries

choose a chain to be delivered, which will be accepted by all miners in the next round. However, in the current round, the following two kinds of chains must be delivered: the chain marked as *non-delayed* and the chain marked as *delayed* for upper-bounded number of rounds.

To analyze the security of blockchain against these attacks, many researchers have tried to investigate various tools and methods. The Markov Decision Process (MDP) model is a typical analysis method. The authors in [19] try to use the MDP model as an analytical tool to evaluate the impact of the selfish mining and double spending attacks in blockchain. Their research results show that the selfish mining and double spending attacks are not rational choices compared with the honest mining strategy. The long delay attack is analyzed in [20]. From these studies, we have learned that the attackers in blockchain systems are mostly rational and aim to maximize their in-system utility, which is the an implicit assumption. Our analysis model is also based on this assumption. We also notice that the above studies set network delay as a constant system parameter in their analysis. It is because the MDP model cannot capture the dynamic network delay. In this work, we will analyze the security of a blockchain system against the long delay attack in dynamic network environment where the partially observable MDP model (POMDP) can serve as a suitable theoretical basis.

2.2. Preliminaries of POMDP

A partially observable Markov decision process (POMDP) can be described by a tuple $< S, A, T, R, O >$. Here S is a set of states; A is a set of decision actions; T is the state transition function which represents the probability of state transferring from current state s to next state s'; R is the reward function $R(s, a)$;

Ω is a set of observations obtained after taking an action; O is the observation function that specifies the probability distribution over observations. Since some states are always partially observable, POMDP maintains a belief state b which is a probability distribution over states. The belief state can be updated according to Eq.(1) as action a is taken and observation o is observed.

$$b'(s')=\Pr(s'|o,a,b)=\frac{\Pr(o|s',a)}{\Pr(o|b,a)}\sum_s \Pr(s'|s,a)b(s)$$

(1)

The goal of the POMDP model is to find the best strategy to maximize the action-taker's reward, but the parameters to calculate the expected reward are usually unknown. There are many ways to learn these parameters. Here we mainly introduce the Bayesian-based learning method. In the Bayesian learning process, the Dirichlet distribution is used to represent the probability distribution of the model parameters. $O_{s'a}$ denotes the probability distribution of the observed value under state s' and execution action a. We assume that both the prior and posterior distributions are Dirichlet distributions, where $\phi_{O_i}^{s'a}$ is the Dirichlet parameter. Then the prior distribution can be calculated according to [21], as is described in Eq.(2).

$$\Pr(o_i|s',a)=\frac{\phi_{O_i}^{s'a}}{\sum_{n=1}^{|\Omega|}\phi_{O_i}^{s'a}}$$

(2)

On the basis of the prior distribution, the posterior distribution is updated given a series of observation history. Let $h_{s'a}$ denote a set of observations when action a causes a state transition to state s', and $N(o_i|h_{s'a})$ be the number of times observation o_i appears in $h_{s'a}$, then the posterior probability of $Q_{s'a}$ can be calculated according to Eq.(3)

$$\Pr(o_i|s',a)=\frac{\phi_{O_i}^{s'a} + N(o_i\,|\,h_{s'a})}{\sum_{n=1}^{|\Omega|}[\phi_{O_i}^{s'a} + N(o_i\,|\,h_{s'a})]} \tag{3}$$

In general, the observation functions of the POMDP model should be customized in different application environments. In our model, the observation function of POMDP needs to be learned based on a clustering algorithm.

3. THE PROPOSED ANALYSIS MODEL

The target of our model is to analyze the security of a blockchain system against the long delay attack, through evaluating the optimized rewards of the attackers. It is assumed that the attackers are rational and always aim to maximize their utility. Our analysis model consists of two main modules as is shown in Figure 1. The first module is the POMDP model for attackers in optimizing the long-delay strategy of attackers in a blockchain system under evaluation. The six components of the POMDP model are specified, including a clustering method to learn the observation function of the network delay in the real time. The second module is the security analysis method by comparing the rewards of the attackers and honest miners. The evaluated system is regarded to be safe against the long

9

delay attack if the rewards of the attackers based on our POMDP model are no more than those of honest miners.

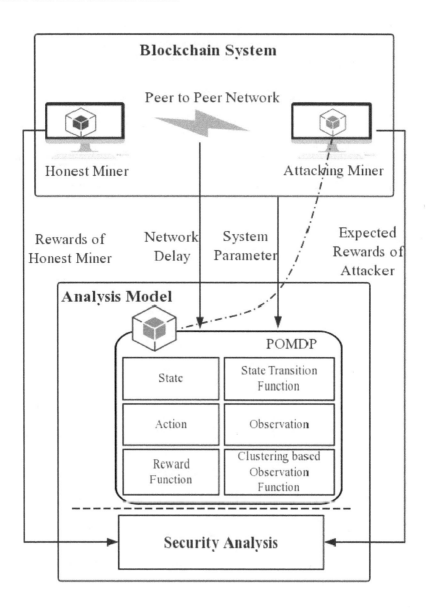

Figure 1: The Proposed Analysis Model

3.1. Problem Formalization and Assumptions

The main parameters in our model and their notions are explained in Table 1.

Term	Notation	Explaination
Mining power	α	the fraction of nodes controlled by adversaries over total number of miner nodes.
Mining cost	c_m	the cost paid by miners for mining blocks
Delay cost	c_d	the cost paid by the adversary for launching the long delay attac
Network delay	Δ	the additional mining time gained by attacker through delay attack.
Network delay bound	Δ_{total}	the maximum network delay allowed by the system.
Time window	W	a period of time and attackers may perform multiple delay attacks in each time window
Benefits of attackers	R_a	expected total benefit of an attacker performing long delay attack in W
Benefits of miners	R_h	expected total benefit of honest miners.
Block reward	R_b	rewards received by the wining miner for each new block
Mining hardness	$p = 1 / c\Delta$	indicating how hard it is to mine a block and c is the mining hardness paramete

Table 1: Notation Summary

Note that our model needs to assume that the attackers are rational, which leads to our settings about the attacker: The attacker will try to get the maximum benefit that an attacker can get in a period of time as much as possible. This is because we guarantee the security of the blockchain on the condition that any profit of the attacker can't be greater than the honest profit. So, it's reasonable that we should get the maximum profit of the attacker under this condition. On the basis of the settings about the attacker, we have made rules on how attackers can execute long delay attacks. These rules are designed to limit the behavior of attackers in our model, so as to prevent the infinite waste of resources. The behavior of infinite waste of resources includes infinite execution of observation action, which can consume the attacker's resources, but can not bring benefits to the attacker. In our model, the behavior of the attacker is spec-ified as follows: The attacker will perform a limited number of query operations in each decision-making process. The attacker will choose whether to attack or not according to the strategy he chooses at each time We will accumulate the benefits of the attacker's choice at all times.

In our model, through launching the delay attack, the attacker can gain additional time to mine the next block in advance. Thus, once the delay attack is launched successfully, the probability of successfully mining the next new block becomes higher than normal miners.

Let T_1 denote the time a new block takes from being created to being received by an attacker. Similarly, we denote T_2 as the processing time taken by the attacker in validating the block. In the setting of static network delay, T_1 and T_2 are

12

constants. Given the information transmission upper bound Δ_{total}, we can calculate the delay time Δ left for the attacker, which is also a constant.

$$\Delta = \Delta_{total} - T_1 - T_2 \tag{4}$$

In a dynamic network, the value of T_1 becomes dynamic while T_2 and Δ_{total} could still be constant values. Thus, Δ is also dynamic with the real-time network status.

Given the mining hardness p, the number of blocks the attacker can mine in the period of Δ is $\alpha p\Delta$[7]. When $\alpha p\Delta > 1$, the attacker can always mine a new block in performing the long delay attack. Moreover, the long delay attack itself has a success rate a [13]. Therefore, when the attacker executes a delay attack, the probability of successfully extending the attacker's chain by 1 is $a\alpha p\Delta$. This is also the reason why the probability of successfully launching the delay attack will be reduced in the case of high network delay. In our model, as Δ changes with the network status, the attacker may not always successfully mine a new block in an attack. That is, even after the successful execution of the delay attack, the attacker may be unable to successfully extend his own chain by 1. For simplification, our model considers the network delay status as two discrete levels: the high delay and the low delay, respectively.

Our model will measure the total optimal rewards R_a for an attacker in a time window W, then compare R_a with the expected rewards of an honest miner R_h. There could be several delay attack rounds in each time window and an attacker may execute multiple attacks in every round. The attacker divides a round into k

fragments and delays all messages received in a whole fragment: from the start to the end of the fragment. The delay of each message shall not exceeds Δ.

Next, we are to introduce the two parts of our analysis model.

3.2. POMDP Components

The object of our POMDP module is to optimize the strategy of attackers in performing the long delay attack. There are six components in our POMDP module, namely state, action, state transition function, reward function, observation, and observation function. We then specify every component as follow.

3.2.1. State

The state of POMDP is denoted by $S = <n, l>$, containing two types of states. The first one is network delay state $n \in \{High, Low\}$, and the second one is the relative length $l \in \{0,1,2,...\}$ of the chain hold by the attacker to the longest chain of honest miners. The network delay state has two possible values, with High and Low corresponds the situation of high delay and low delay in the overall system respectively. The relative length state is a non-negative integer, computed as the length of the attacker's own chain minus that of the honest chain. The relative length cannot be negative because the attacker can observe the honest chain and update its chain to the equal length before adding its delayed blocks. Note that the relative length will be reset to 0 after each delay attack round.

3.2.2. Action

An attacker can choose an action a from an action set A which contains three types of actions, i.e. A = {*Query, Attack, Wait*}. The first action is *Query*, which is the action of the attacker to obtain the observation information from the system. It should be noted that in our model the information received directly from the system needs to be processed in our model which will be specified later, and the query action represents a continuous process from the execution of the action to information procession. The second action is *Attack*. Executing an *Attack* action means that the attacker chooses to launch the delay attack in the current time fragment. The third is *Wait*, where the attacker gives up performing the long delay attacks in the current time.

3.2.3. State Transition Function

The general expression of the state transition function is $Pr(s' =< n', l' > |s =< n, l >, a)$. Through executing *Query* action, the action-taker can update its network delay state $s \rightarrow s'$ according to the network observations, but the relative length l should not be updated.

For an Attack action, the relative length l can be updated by $l+1$ when the attack is performed successfully, but the network delay status keep the same. The success rate depends on the network delay state. Specifically, when the network is in high delay, the success rate is denoted by $Pr(s' =< high, l' > |s =< high, l >, A) = S$. When the network is in low delay, the success rate is $Pr(s' =< low, l'$

$> |s =< low,l >,A) = D$. According to the nature of the long delay attack, the value of D should be greater than S. The state transition functions when $a = Attack$ are described as Eqs.(5) and (6)

$$Pr(< high, l' > | < high, l >, Attack) = \begin{cases} S & l' = l +1 \\ 1 - S & l' = l -1 \\ 0 & others \end{cases} \quad (5)$$

$$Pr(< low, l' > | < low, l >, Attack) = \begin{cases} D & l' = l +1 \\ 1 - D & l' = l -1 \\ 0 & others \end{cases} \quad (6)$$

For the Wait action, the network state should not be changed. The relative length of the chain has two possible states: $l' = l$ or $l' = l -1$. When $l' = l$, there is no new block generated, the chain length of attackers and honest miners are unchanged, the probability is denoted by $Pr(< n,l > | < n,l >, Wait) = H$. When $l' = l -1$, a new block is mined by an honest miner but the long delay attacker losses the chance of mining the same level block.

$$Pr(< n, l' > | < n, l >, Wait) = \begin{cases} H & l' = l \\ 1 - H & l' = l -1 \\ 0 & others \end{cases} \quad (7)$$

3.2.4. Reward Function

For *Query* action, an attacker has to take a certain amount of time to update his network status, and it will result in the cost R_q.

$$Pr(< low, l' > | < low, l >, Query) = R_q \quad (8)$$

For *Attack* action, when the relative length increases by 1, the attacker is rewarded by R_a. When the relative length decreases by 1, the attacker is punished by R_d.

16

$$Pr(< n, l' > \mid < n, l >, Attack) = \begin{cases} R_q + R_q - c_m - c_d & l' = l \ + 1 \\ -R_q - c_m - c_d & l' = l \ - 1 \\ 0 & others \end{cases} \quad (9)$$

where c_m is the mining cost and c_d is the delay cost, and R_b is the block rewards.

For the *Wait* action, keeping the relative length unchanged will not be punished,

nor be rewarded $R(s' > |s, W) = 0$. However, if the network delay state is in a low

delay state and the attacker still chooses to wait, the attacker will

be punished R_z.

$$Pr(< n, l' > \mid < n, l >, Wait) = \begin{cases} 0 & l' = l \\ -R_z & l' = l \ - 1 \\ 0 & others \end{cases} \quad (10)$$

3.2.5. Observation

When the attacker performs a query action, the current network delay states of

every connected nodes are obtained. The observed value o_n has two possible

values {*high, low*} , denoting high delay network status and low delay network

respectively. Due to the nature of peer-to-peer blockchain network, each node can

only judge its own neighboring network status. Thus, we have to aggregate the

received observations to predict the system network status.

3.2.6. Observation Function

The state can only be observed when query actions are executed. An observation

function is generally expressed as $Pr(o \mid s', Query)$. In our model, the network delay

state is partially observable, and the relative length state is completely observable.

The essence of observation function learning is how to judge the current network situation based on the previous observation history and current observation results. We need to note that our model aims to determine the network observation of the whole system, instead of only considering its connected nodes.

3.3. Belief Function Update

POMDP maintains a belief state b which is a probability distribution over states. If $b(s)$ represents the probability that the world is instate s, the updated belief state $b(s)$ is calculated every time any action a is taken and observation o is received.

$$b'(s') = Pr(s'\,|\,o,a,b) = \frac{Pr(o\,|\,s',a)}{Pr(o\,|\,b,a)} \sum_s Pr(s'\,|\,s,a)b(s)$$

Given the observation $o = o_n$, current state $s = n$ and the next state $s = n'$, the belief update is given by

$$b'(n') \propto Pr(o\,|\,s',Q)\sum_s Pr(s'\,|\,s,Q)b(s)$$

We can learn from the state transition function that in the case of $n' = n$, the state transition function after executing the query action. Therefore
the belief update is now given by

$$b'(n') \propto Pr(o\,|\,s',Q)b(s)$$

Next, we'll show how to learn observation functions $Pr(o\,|\,s',Q)$ in detail.

3.4. Learning Observation Function

In practice, the network environment is constantly changing. As a result, our model can not be in a static state. The observation function of our model needs to be adjusted with the network state at all times. Therefore, in our POMDP model, the generation of observation function is a learning process.

We know that the network condition is an extremely difficult attribute to observe. To achieve the observation of the network condition, we use the historical observation records as an auxiliary. Specifically, the observation results of each node obtained by the attacker through multiple query actions are collected in a specified period to constitute the observation history set. Dirichlet distribution $Dir^{s'}(\phi_{o_n}^{s'}, o_n \in \{high, low\})$ is initialized by using observation history set.

Giving the history of the number of observations, the posterior probability of the occurrence of observations can be calculated according to the number of times $o_n = high$ and $o_n = low$ which appear in the observation history. So far, we have obtained the posterior probability for each observation.

In fact, the sum of a pair of posterior probabilities is one, so we can use only one posterior probability to represent the observation status at each time $Pr(o_n = high \mid s')$. We add a timestamp to each posterior probability to indicate the number of rounds it generates. Thus a posterior probability vector $(Pr, t1)$ is formed. Each observation will form such a vector. After a period of time and several rounds of observation, we get a set of posterior probability vectors and use it for K-Means clustering analysis.

One dimension of K-Means clustering is the time dimension, which represents the observation time. The longer the observation time, the closer the observation time is. Another dimension of clustering is the posterior probability, which reflects the judgment of network status in the current system.

After clustering, we select the nearest category C and obtain the observation function by getting the center of C .It can be used to initialize a new POMDP model which will be able to reflect current network latency state.

In the Bitcoin network, each node will be connected to other nodes, the minimum number is 8, and the general average is 32[15]. This means that each node can learn about the network latency associated with it, but this understandingis very limited. For attackers, it is very important to understand the network latency of the whole network. Therefore, an attacker needs a method to integratthe information of each node and aggregate it into the network delay status ofthe whole network. In fact, we draw an effective time range by clustering. Thefunction of clustering is to grasp the general features of network changes in acertain period of time. By learning this feature, we can Learn the probabilityof getting observations. That's why we use clustering.

3.5. Security Analysis Metric

In this part, we will use the data from the POMDP parts to analyze the security of a blockchain system. We assume that in time W, the expected reward of the attacker is E_a which is calculated by the POMDP model. At the same time, within the same time W, the expected reward of honest miners is E_h given the block

reward being R_b .

If the reward of the attacker is greater than that of honesty at the same time, that

is

$$E_a > E_h$$

then our model decides that there is a security risk in this blockchain system.

Because it is possible for an attacker to choose to execute the delay attack in order

to maximize his own interests. On the other hand, if the benefit of attack is less

than that of honesty at the same time, that is

$$E_a < E_h$$

Then our model will determine that the blockchain system is secure. For rational

attackers, in order to maximize their own interests, they will not choose to engage

in hard and low-yielding behavior like launching the attack.

4. EXPERIMENTS

In this section, we will mainly introduce our experiments. We have executed two

kinds of experiments. The first kind is the comparison of the effects of several

strategies. This includes our POMDP, the greedy strategy and some other

intelligent strategies. In the second kind of experiments, we mainly study the

influence of some parameters of blockchain system.The main purpose of our

experiments is to verify the superiority and validity of our model. In addition, on

the basis of superiority and validity, we use our model to analyze the security performance of the blockchain system under different parameters. On this basis, the expected reward of the attacker will be compared with those of honest mining. Next, before we introduce our experiments, we will introduce our simulation setup.

4.1. Simulation Setup

In this section, we will explain various settings used in our experiment.

The first is the basic input of the experiment. The input of the experimentis provided by the simulator. We used the blockchain simulator[19] to evaluate our POMDP model, which is based on NS3. In order to simulate the real environment, we choose the Bitcoin environment as our simulation object. The parameters of our simulation environment will be consistent with Bitcoin. It includes block size and block generation time.There are two reasons for choosing the simulator instead of real Bitcoin environment. One is that it is convenient for us to obtain the output. The other is that it is convenient for us to adjust the parameters of the blockchain system at any time.

Then, the direct output from the simulator needs further processing to work on our model. In our model, when the network delay given by the node is greater than the average of the same group, we think that the node is in a high network delay; when the network delay given by the point is less than the average of the same group, we think that the node is in a low network delay. The network delay given by the node is determined by the timestamp of the message received by the node.

These are all the settings of our experiment. Next we will introduce our two kinds of experiments

4.2. The First Experiment: Evaluation of The Proposed Security Analysis Model

In this kind of experiment, in order to show the superiority of our model, we let attackers use three different strategies to attack. These three strategies are our model, the Greedy strategy and some intelligent strategies without consid ering dynamic network delay. The Greedy strategy is a common strategy chosen by attackers. Because of unclear or unable to obtain the network conditions in the blockchain system, attackers have to carry out as many attacks as possible to ensure that their attacks work, so as to obtain the maximum benefits. The intelligent strategy is based on the greedy strategy. Because there are many uncertainties in the blockchain system, it is not likely to obtain the maximum benefit by blindly attacking. Therefore, many researchers[19] have studied how to attack, so there will be some intelligent strategies to help attackers to make decisions. The intelligent strategy which does not support dynamic network delay observation generally refers to the policy which sets the network delay to

be constant or does not consider the network delay. There are some reasons for putting different intelligent strategies into one category: On the one hand, due to the compression of blockchain security in our previous analysis, at present we focus on the ability of blockchain consistency. On this basis, we analyzed a variety of attacks against the consistency of the blockchain and made a brief

23

overview, and finally chose the long delay attack that seems most likely to affect the blockchain system. This makes the other means of attacks ignored by us. On the other hand, as far as we know, we are the first to adopt the intelligent strategy of dynamic network delay modeling and analysis. This situation makes our opponents, who basically set the blockchain network delay as a constant and do not care about the network delay, and basically can not accurately obtain the network delay information when analyzing our simulation environment. Their judgment on the network delay has nothing to do with the strategy itself. Based on the above two points, we classify these strategies into one class and compare them with our POMDP model. The experimental results are shown in Figure 2. When the network state is in frequent transition between high and low latency, we call this network state network fluctuation state. In this state, the benefits of the other two strategies will be greatly reduced, which is also because they can not better judge the change of network state. And the benefits of our strategy will grow steadily.

In summary, we can see that our model can more accurately reflect the attacker's benefits under the dynamic network delay changes. And our model can get the best benefits of attackers. This will be the basis for our next blockchain security analysis.

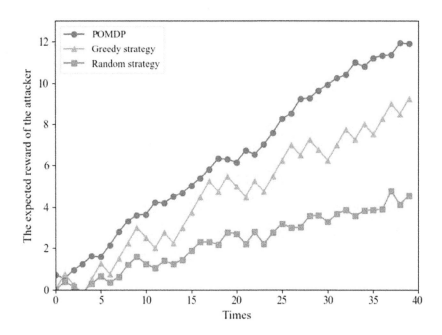

Figure 2: The Rewards of Attackers with Different Attacking Strategies

4.3. The Second Experiment: Impact of Different Blockchain Parameters

In this section, we will use our model to analyze the impact of blockchain parameters on blockchain security. We will analyze the following parameters: the mining hardness of the blockchain system, the network delay bound and the mining power of the attacker. Mining hardness in the blockchain system means the difficulty for a miner to successfully mine a block. This parameter is generally pre-designed, global, and dynamically adjusted. The network delay bound reflects the maximum delay upper bound allowed by the system when miners deliver messages in the blockchain system. Messages beyond this upper bound will no longer be considered valid. Similar to mining hardness, this parameter is pre-designed and usually does not change. The mining power of the attacker is the parameter that can most affect the security of the blockchain system. The higher the mining power of the attacker is, the higher the success rate of executing the attack would be. Generally, considering the Byzantine fault tolerance of blockchain system, we think that the mining power of attackers will not account for more than half.

4.3.1. Impact of the Mining Hardness

ob represents the network environment parameters. The closer ob is to 0.5, the more unstable the network condition is. In the experimental results, we give three values of ob to represent the three situations of network state. The network is relatively stable, the network is relatively unstable, and the network is quite unstable.

According to the network delay relationship mentioned before, the difficulty of mining hardness changes will affect the success rate of attackers in high delay and low delay situations. With the increase of difficulty p, the success rate of an attacker is also increasing. Moreover, when the mining difficulty increases to a certain value, the attacker's expected reward will tend to be a constant value. Figure 3 presents the specific results. Combined with the results in the Figure3, the safety range of mining difficulty given by us is 0.7-0.9 when considering as many network cases as possible.

4.3.2. Impact of Network Delay Bound

The network delay bound of the system will also affect the benefits of the attack. With the increase of the network delay limit of the system, the attacker will get more time to attack, which will increase the probability of a successful delay attack. In this part, we first need to quantify the increase of network delay bound. We mentioned in the previous analysis that the time allowed for attackers to launch the delay attack Δ is determined by the delay in the network and the network delay boundΔ_{total}. After initializing the attacker's other parameters, we use a network delay parameter h to express the increasing network delay bound. With the increase of the network delay bound, Δ gradually increases to $h\square$. Figure 4 will specifically reflect the impact of this change on the expected reward of the attacker.

Combined with the results in the Figure 4, the safety range of the network delay bound given by us is 0.7-0.9 when considering as many network cases as possible.

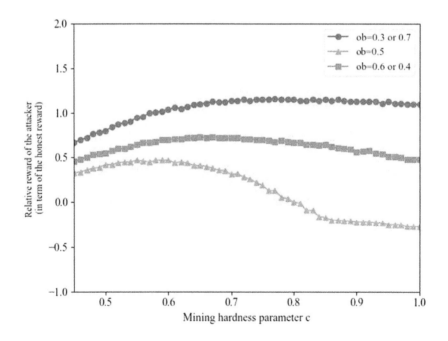

Figure 3: The Rewards of Attackers with Varied Mining Hardness

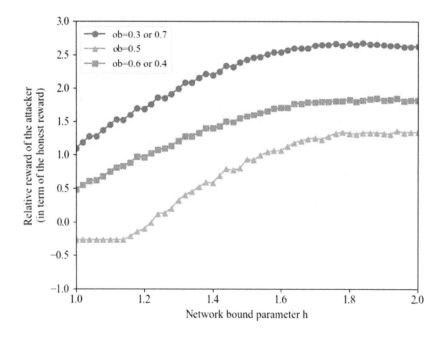

Figure 4: The Rewards of Attackers with Varied Network Delay Bound

4.3.3. Impact of Mining Power

In addition to the above two blockchain system parameters, the attack's own mining power will also affect its success rate of delay attack as is shown in Figure 5. Moreover, the attacker's mining power also affects the attacker's profit in the honest state. Combined with the results in the Figure 5, the safety range of the mining power given by us is 0.7-0.9 when considering as many network cases as possible.

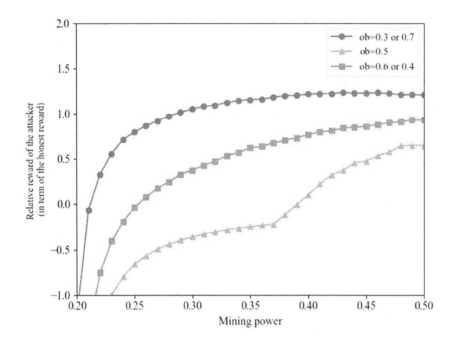

Figure 5: The Rewards of Attackers with Varied Mining Power

4.4. Final Result Analysis

In general, the blockchain system should ensure that the attacker with less than 50% mining power should not always successfully mine a block in the Δ time. To ensure this, the blockchain system needs to set a lower network delay limit Δ_{total} and relatively difficult mining difficulty p. That means keeping $\Box \alpha p < 1$. The specific parameter range can refer to our results.

5. CONCLUSION AND FUTURE WORK

We build an analysis model to analyze the security of a blockchain system facing the delay attack. Our model is mainly based on the POMDP model and uses cluster analysis to provide the observation function for POMDP. We can judge whether the blockchain system is secure by comparing the gap between the attacker's expected reward in the attack state and the honest state. We have carried out many experiments in the simulation environment and found the security range of some parameters in the BitCoin blockchain system that is similar to the analyzed results.

In our analysis model, we focus on the delay attack. In fact, the attacks against the data consistency of blockchain can be more complex than the delay attack. A blockchain system may face different attacking scenarios. In future work, we will try to integrate other attacking scenarios into our analysis model. Finally, our model can be general and suitable enough for analyzing a complicate blockchain system. In addition, the parameters of several blockchain systems mentioned in this paper actually have a certain relationship with the data performance of blockchain. Sometimes the security performance and data performance of blockchain are likely to be antagonistic with each other. We will add the impact factors on blockchain data performance in analyzing blockchain system security in our future work.

ACKNOWLEDGEMENT:This work is supported in part by the National Natural Science Foundation for Young Scientists of China under Grant No.61702090 and No. 61702084. 111 Project (B16009) of Key Laboratory of Data Analytics and Optimization for Smart Industry (Northeastern University), Ministry of Education, China

REFERENCES

1. S. Nakamoto, Bitcoin: A peer-to-peer electronic cash system, https:// bitcoin.org/bitcoin.pdf (2008).

2. M. Crosby, P. Pattanayak, S. Verma, V. Kalyanaraman, et al., Blockchain technology: Beyond bitcoin, Applied Innovation 2 (6-10) (2016) 71.

3. M. Swan, Blockchain: Blueprint for a new economy, " O'Reilly Media, Inc.", 2015.

4. Q. Xia, E. B. Sifah, K. Huang, R. Chen, X. Du, J. Gao, Secure payment routing protocol for economic systems based on blockchain, in: Proceedings of the International Conference on Computing, Networking and Communi cations, 2018, pp. 177–181.

5. T. Dey, S. Jaiswal, S. Sunderkrishnan, N. Katre, Healthsense: A medical use case of internet of things and blockchain, in: Proceedings of the Inter national Conference on Intelligent Sustainable Systems, 2017, pp. 486–491.

6. C. Alexopoulos, Y. Charalabidis, A. Androutsopoulou, M. A. Lout saris, Z. Lachana, Benefits and obstacles of blockchain applications in e government, in: Proceedings of 52nd Hawaii International Conference on System Sciences, HICSS, 2019, pp. 1–10.

7. R. Pass, L. Seeman, A. Shelat, Analysis of the blockchain protocol in asynchronous networks, in: Proceedings of Annual International Conferences on the Theory and Applications of Cryptographic Techniques, 2017, pp. 643–673.

8. L. Bach, B. Mihaljevic, M. Zagar, Comparative analysis of blockchain consensus algorithms, in: 2018 41st International Convention on Information and Communication Technology, Electronics and Microelectronics (MIPRO), IEEE, 2018, pp. 1545–1550.

9. X. Li, P. Jiang, T. Chen, X. Luo, Q. Wen, A survey on the security of blockchain systems, Future Generation Computer Systems 107 (2020) 841–853.

10. M. Alaslani, F. Nawab, B. Shihada, Blockchain in iot systems: End-to-end delay evaluation, IEEE Internet of Things Journal 6 (5) (2019) 8332–8344.

11. Y. Aoki, K. Otsuki, T. Kaneko, R. Banno, K. Shudo, Simblock: Ablockchain network simulator, in: IEEE Conference on Computer Communications Workshops, IEEE, 2019, pp. 325–329.

12. C. Pinz´on, C. Rocha, J. Finke, Algorithmic analysis of blockchain efficiency with communication delay, in: H. Wehrheim, J. Cabot (Eds.), 23rd International Conference on Fundamental Approaches to Software Engineering, Vol. 12076 of Lecture Notes in Computer Science, pp. 400–419.

13. P. Wei, Q. Yuan, Y. Zheng, Security of the blockchain against long delay attack, in: Proceedings of 24th International Conference on the Theory and Application of Cryptology and Information Security, 2018, pp. 250–275.

14. Q. Yuan, P. Wei, K. Jia, H. Xue, Analysis of blockchain protocol against static adversarial miners corrupted by long delay attackers, Science China Information Science 63 (3).

15. C. Decker, R. Wattenhofer, Information propagation in the bitcoin network, in: Proceedings of the 13th IEEE International Conference on Peer-to-Peer Computing, 2013, pp. 1–10.

16. E. Androulaki, A. Barger, V. Bortnikov, C. Cachin, K. Christidis, A. De Caro, D. Enyeart, C. Ferris, G. Laventman, Y. Manevich, et al., Hyperledger fabric: a distributed operating system for permissioned blockchains, in: Proceedings of the Thirteenth EuroSys Conference, 2018, pp. 1–15.

17. I. Eyal, E. G. Sirer, Majority is not enough: Bitcoin mining is vulnerable, in: Proceedings of International Conference on Financial Cryptography and Data Security, 2014, pp. 436–454.

18. C. Badertscher, J. A. Garay, U. Maurer, D. Tschudi, V. Zikas, But why does it work? A rational protocol design treatment of bitcoin, in: Proceedings of the 37th Annual International Conference on the Theory and Applications of Cryptographic Techniques, 2018, pp. 34–65

19. A. Gervais, G. O. Karame, K. Wu¨st, V. Glykantzis, H. Ritzdorf, S. Cap kun, On the security and performance of proof of work blockchains, in: Proceedings of ACM SIGSAC Conference on Computer and Communications Security, 2016, pp. 3–16.

20. L. Kiffer, R. Rajaraman, a. shelat, A better method to analyze blockchain consistency, in: Proceedings of the ACM SIGSAC Conference on Computer and Communications Security, 2018, pp. 729–744.

21. S. Ross, B. Chaib-draa, J. Pineau, Bayesian reinforcement learning in continuous pomdps with application to robot navigation, in: Proceedings of

IEEE International Conference on Robotics and Automation, 2008, pp. 2845–2851.

CONTENTS

Publisher: Eliva Press SRL

Email: info@elivapress.com

Eliva Press is an independent publishing house established for the publication and dissemination of academic works all over the world. Company provides high quality and professional service for all of our authors.

Our Services:
Free of charge, open-minded, eco-friendly, innovational.

-All services are free of charge for you as our author (manuscript review, step-by-step book preparation, publication, distribution, and marketing).
-No financial risk. The author is not obliged to pay any hidden fees for publication.
-Editors. Dedicated editors will assist step by step through the projects.
-Money paid to the author for every book sold. Up to 50% royalties guaranteed.
-ISBN (International Standard Book Number). We assign a unique ISBN to every Eliva Press book.
-Digital archive storage. Books will be available online for a long time. We don't need to have a stock of our titles. No unsold copies. Eliva Press uses environment friendly print on demand technology that limits the needs of publishing business. We care about environment and share these principles with our customers.
-Cover design. Cover art is designed by a professional designer.
-Worldwide distribution. We continue expanding our distribution channels to make sure that all readers have access to our books.

www.elivapress.com

www.ingramcontent.com/pod-product-compliance
Lightning Source LLC
LaVergne TN
LVHW052125070326
832902LV00038B/3950

Yuan Liu is an associate professor at Software College, Northeastern University in Shenyang China. She received her B.Eng degree in the honor school, Harbin Institute of Technology, China, in 2010. She achieved her Ph.D degree in School of Computer Engineering from Nanyang Technological University (NTU), Singapore, in 2014. From 2014 to 2015, she ever worked as Research Fellow at Joint NTU-UBC Research Centre of Excellence in Active Living for the Elderly (LILY), NTU, Singapore. Her research interests include blockchain consensus protocols, trust-based incentive mechanism design, multi-agent system, trust management, blockchain technology based reputation systems. Her research papers have been published in top international conferences in the area of blockchain and artificial intelligence.

Blockchain is a distributed ledger, offering an innovative approach to establishing trust in a public and open environment. However, it bears many security attacks in sustaining data/status consistency in the process of data storing and exchanging, and the long-delay attack is one of the most challenging ones. Many researchers have adopted various methods in analyzing the blockchain system security by considering a upper-bounded and static network latency. In a realistic scenario, the network latency is always changing dynamically, resulting in the unreliability and inaccuracy of the existing analysis approaches. In this book, we propose a blockchain security analysis model based on partially observable Markov decision process (POMDP) against the long delay attack by capturing the dynamic network delay. In our model, an observation function about the network delay is learned and updated based on a clustering algorithm according to the real-time network status. With the support of the observation function, a POMDP model is constructed for attackers to maximize their expected rewards. To analyze the security of a blockchain system against the long delay attack, the utility of the attackers and normal miners with the same mining power is calculated and compared. The system is safe as the utility of the normal miners is no less than that of the attackers. Extensive experiments are conducted to show the effectiveness of the proposed analysis model, where Bitcoin system is evaluated and the safe ranges of the system network parameters are analyzed.

www.elivapress.com

ISBN 978-1-952751-33-2